OCEAN CITY

Ocean City Memories

Kind Regards

David Trozzo

1990

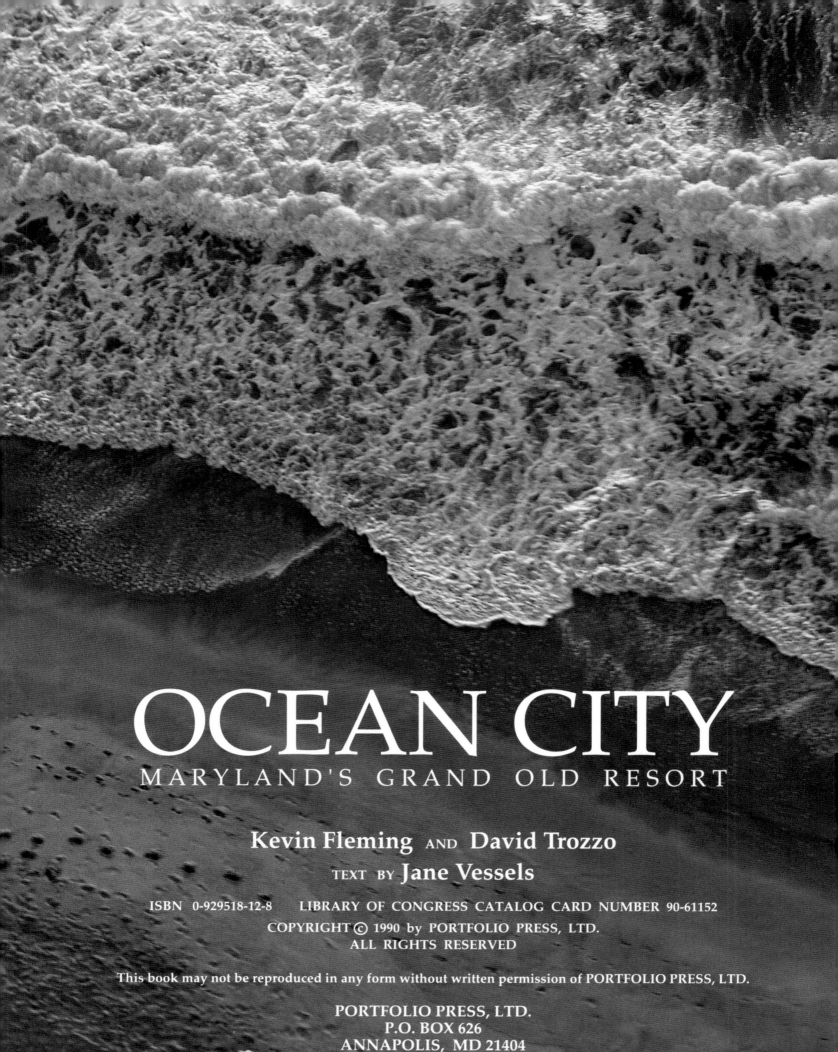

OCEAN CITY
MARYLAND'S GRAND OLD RESORT

Kevin Fleming AND **David Trozzo**
TEXT BY **Jane Vessels**

ISBN 0-929518-12-8   LIBRARY OF CONGRESS CATALOG CARD NUMBER 90-61152

COPYRIGHT © 1990 by PORTFOLIO PRESS, LTD.

PORTFOLIO PRESS, LTD.
P.O. BOX 626
ANNAPOLIS, MD 21404
1-800-233-3347

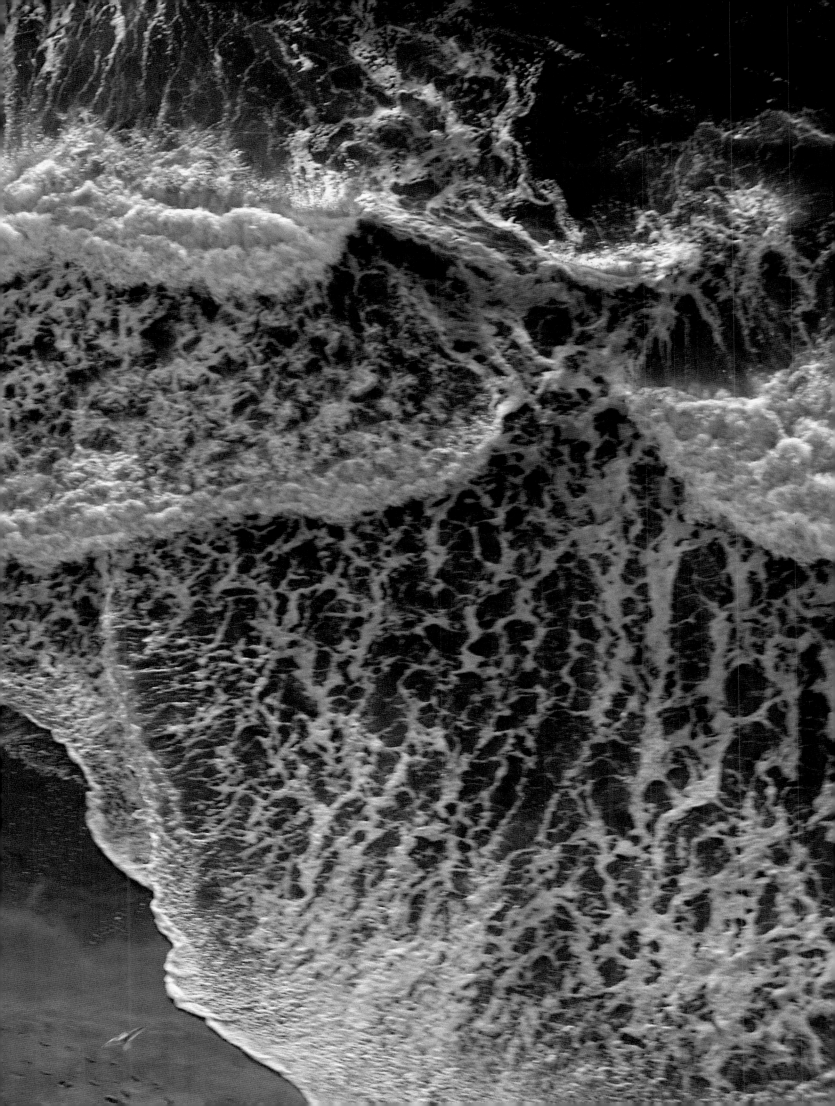

Looking north from the newly-cut inlet, September 1936.

Maryland's Grand Old Resort

A strip of sand trails off Maryland's Atlantic coast like a wisp of hair tossed by a summer breeze. On this shifting barrier island, today ten miles long and at most a mile wide, Ocean City took root after the Civil War. As the nation set about binding its wounds, cultural and economic changes were encouraging bold new concepts: leisure time and outdoor recreation.

Taking a chance on these trends, investors from the Eastern Shore, Baltimore, and Philadelphia formed the Atlantic Hotel Company Corporation in 1868 to develop an ocean resort in rural Worcester County. They optioned 50 acres from Stephen Taber, a New York resident with local ties, who called his land "Ladies Resort to the Ocean." With Atlantic City

already taken as a place name, the corporation considered calling its gamble Beach City or Sinepuxent City, before choosing Ocean City.

On July 4, 1875, at least 800 people, including members of the press, boated across the bay to the barrier island for the opening of the 400-room Atlantic Hotel, "a marvel in architectural beauty." Through their business connections, the developers had secured a short extension of the Wicomico and Pocomoke Railroad from the town of Berlin to the western shore of Sinepuxent Bay. The next year, a railroad bridge linked island to mainland, and Ocean City was launched.

On July 4, 1989, 340,000 vacationers – dressed in ways

those first excursionists never imagined – set a new Ocean City visitor record. The lodestone of Maryland tourism now draws nearly eight million people a year, some three million of them during what was once called the off-season.

The high-rise Ocean City they see is a recent chapter in the resort's history. The island didn't hold a building taller than ten stories before the 1970s, when explosive development created a profile reminiscent of Miami Beach. On the northern stretch, condominiums of twenty-plus stories march toward the Delaware border. Sleek midrise hotels at the island's center give way to smaller inns and wooden apartment houses on the southern end, where the resort had its beginnings. And in the midst of 35,000 rooms for rent are the homes of 8,500 people who live here year-round.

There is dissension in the community today. Some residents, mainly newcomers, have taken a pull-up-the-bridge attitude and want development to stop. The majority, learning from the past, want careful growth that benefits home-town Ocean City yet keeps in sight the reason it was created: vacations.

The first visitors were Naticokes and other Indians who fished and hunted on this island they called Assateague, the "place across." In January 1650, Indians came to the aid of English colonist Henry Norwood, put ashore here to find fresh water, then unaccountably abandoned by his Virginia-bound ship. By the 1750s, European settlers had pushed all but a handful of

Indians from the Eastern Shore. Assateague became a seasonal grazing ground for livestock, ferried to the island each spring.

Ocean City parted violently with Assateague Island when a hurricane slashed an inlet in 1933. Overnight, the bulk of Assateague lay to the inlet's south, and

A postcard circa 1910 recalls an era when a man without a bathing suit top would have been scandalous (top). In this 1909 postcard the Pier was two years old.

Ocean City became the southern terminus of Fenwick Island, named for 17th-century landowner Thomas Fenwick.

On the land swept out to sea in the inlet's creation, two rough cottages (Isaac Coffin's 1869 Rhode Island Inn and James Massey's 1872 rooming house) had accomodated visiting surf fishermen even before

the grand Atlantic Hotel rose nearby. Farther south on Assateague at Green Run Bay, Scott's Ocean House had also opened in 1869. Popular with the Baltimore-Washington-Philadelphia crowd through the 1880s, it closed in the face of competition from Ocean City and its direct rail service.

Three hotels, assorted cottages, and a station of the U.S. Life-Saving Service comprised Ocean City in 1890 when the resort took its next leap, engineered by the Sinepuxent Beach Company of Baltimore City. Buying more of Taber's land north and south of the original resort, these new developers aggressively sold 25-by-142-foot lots, "while they last," starting at 25 dollars. Drawing its northern border at 15th Street, the village incorporated in 1894 and elected a mayor from the Sinepuxent Beach Company board.

Ocean City entered the 20th century with more than a dozen large hotels, a growing number of rooming houses, an electric power plant, and 250 year-round residents – enough to open an elementary school. Daniel Trimper's amusement park, the resort's first, had been operating since 1890 near the nascent Boardwalk, which reached Eighth Street by 1897. Social decorum and clothing styles were becoming more relaxed, and more than ever people wanted to be outdoors and active. "In the Good Old Summertime," an instantly popular 1902 vaudeville ballad, expressed a national mood that Ocean City hummed all the way to the bank.

Innkeepers worked hard for that money. Setting a welcoming atmosphere, they met their guests at the train station on Philadelphia Avenue between

A horse-drawn wagon retrieves the catch of pound fishermen in 1911 (top). The men of the U.S. Life-Saving Station were also the resort's first lifeguards and fire fighters.

Wicomico and Somerset. Meals had to be provided—there were virtually no outside restaurants – and the large hotels also maintained ballrooms and game rooms. Many of these hostelries, great and small, were built and managed by women, most of whom had husbands who fished or plied some aspect of the tourist trade. Talk history with any native today and you will be reminded that Ocean City was built by women. "Women ran Ocean City in those days," says 92-year-old Annie Gilligan Bunting, who came here in 1917 and raised three sons and five apartments while her husband served at the local U.S. Coast Guard Station. "And they pretty much do it now."

Ocean City's commerical fishing industry was running strong at the turn of the century, its catch shipped by rail to urban markets as far away as New York. Croaker, porgies, sea trout, and more were taken by a method called pound fishing. Nets were roped around corrals of wooden poles set about a mile offshore. Hand over hand, as their dories pitched in the swells, men hauled in fish by the ton. Muscling the fish-laden boats back to shore through the surf took both skill and nerve. Getting out to sea was not much easier: There was no inlet; rough fishing camps stood where it now flows. The heavy wooden dories were rolled to the ocean on logs or pulled by horses, and launched with a prayer.

Times were roaring on the 1926 Boardwalk, here looking north from North Division Street.

Pound fishing all but died with the creation of the inlet in August, 1933. Amazingly no lives were lost as a three-day hurricane hurled 20-foot-high waves. Nor did these waves directly cut the inlet. The water they pushed across the island overwhelmed the capacity of Sinepuxent Bay, and, in a great earth-moving surge, the water returned to the sea. "You could hear it," recalls Annie Bunting, who rode out the storm in her house a few blocks away.

With this access to safe back-bay dockage, trawlers took over the commerical fishery. More importantly, Ocean City gained a lucrative new tourist pull: sportfishing. In 1939 the resort aclaimed the title White Marlin Capital of the World after a record number of the fighting fish were caught that summer, two of them landed by Franklin Roosevelt on the presidential yacht.

"Ocean City...is held in affection by the whole state, particularly the younger portion," Hulbert Footner wrote in his 1942 traveler's tale, *Maryland Main and the Eastern Shore.* "Children of high-school age sit up until the small hours playing cards or otherwise

The largest marine creature ever seen in Ocean City came in on its own. In March 1922, a snowstorm beached a dead whale in front of the Atlantic Hotel. It was an unexpected diversion for the town's winter residents, and attempts to get rid of it proved to be as memorable. Towed to sea, the whale returned with the tide. Sectioned and hauled to sea, a large part floated back. "Finally in desperation it was blown up with dynamite," reported Mary Ellen Mumford. "A large piece landed on top of the pier and caused a very unpleasant odor when hit by the hot summer sun. Some townspeople say that they were never completely rid of that whale until the pier burned down in 1925."

disporting themselves. This generation simply will not go to bed," he marveled. "On the boardwalk there is a resort called the Beach Club which attracts those a little older in swarms every summer night to drink beer and to dance. Their grandparents would be scandalized to observe the freedom of their manners as the beer releases their inhibitions. What are their parents going to do about it?"

Social changes brought about by World War II did nothing to dampen these summer rites of teenage expression. And in an increasingly affluent society almost every family had a car and many had two. The sea change for Ocean City – and all of the Eastern Shore – came in 1952 when the Cheasapeake Bay Bridge replaced the ferries and cut travel time dramatically. Along with the number of tourists and residents, real-estate values started to rise.

Ocean City's population had reached 1,500 people in 1962, and the city limit had stretched to 45th Street, when a near-hurricane-force northeaster roared down the mid-Atlantic coast. Coinciding with the highest tides of the year, the Ash Wednesday Storm of March 6 and 7 left Ocean City" a world of water," reported the *Baltimore Sun*. Three lives were lost and property damage exceeded 12 million dollars.

But, as in 1933, Ocean City was reborn from a flood. State and federal funds arrived to help rescue Maryland's burgeoning tourist asset. Coinciding with a high tide of demand for waterfront property, a boomtown decade followed.

When excess speculation derailed the high-rise condominium roller coaster in 1974, Ocean City confronted the consequences of that ride. There was good – the new Convention Center was sparking winter tourism. And there was bad – the beach was disappearing.

``The temperature of the sea was perfect, and nothing but the failing twilight called us back to the shore.''

The Atlantic Hotel, Ocean City's first, still welcomes guests at Somerset and the Boardwalk. The building photographed for this 1920 postcard burned in the great fire of 1925 that swept through the power plant, the Pier, and many Boardwalk businesses. Rebuilt, the hotel survived the Ash Wednesday storm of March 1962 that devastated Ocean City and the mid-Atlantic coast.

"Firm and unchangable," is how the Sinepuxent Bay Company promoted this shore in 1892, and no description could be less accurate. Ocean City lies on a barrier island, changable and unstable by nature.

The coast of Maryland lay 100 miles east when the last ice age ended 12,000 years ago. As glaciers melted and the sea level rose, water slowly carried sand

The teenagers of 1910, like generations since, caught the infectious spirit of the shore.

inland. Wind and wave action gradually shaped the barrier islands that now trace the Atlantic coastline and a still-rising sea level nibbles at the beachfront each year.

This continual ocean rise, along with a southward current, relentlessly pushes mid-Atlantic barrier islands toward the mainland. Vivid testimony to this movement is Ocean City's buxom southern beach. A seaward jetty built to stablize the north wall of the inlet has trapped so much sand since 1933 that the city has built a thousand-car parking lot there.

But elsewhere, Fenwick Island was losing ground. The natural dynamics of a barrier island were blocked by a wall of buildings set too close to the sea. As a series of winter storms gnawed at the beach, water

lapped at buildings once protected by a massive sand dune – leveled because it obscured the ocean view.

As the beach eroded, Harry Kelly, Ocean City's energetic mayor from 1970 to 1985, repeatedly bulldozed it back. Today federal backing is helping the city with a longer-term solution to restoring its beach by pumping sand from deep off shore, much as Miami Beach did successfully a decade ago. The great dune will also be recreated.

The foundation of Ocean City, sand is worth the price the resort must pay to keep it – assuring future generations the experience recorded by a visitor in 1892: ``The temperature of the sea was perfect, and nothing but the failing twilight called us back to the shore.''

photographs courtesy of the Ocean City Life-Saving Station Museum

On a quintessential summer day, beach-bound surfers pass an Old Town house decked out for the Fourth of July. Stretching ten miles along Fenwick Island, Ocean City is Maryland's Atlantic resort.

Cut by a hurricane in 1933, the Ocean City Inlet marks the southern border of the peninsular island. Sportfishing boomed in the wake of this new passage linking back bays and sea (following page).

Horizons expand for the price of a quarter along
the pier overlooking the Ocean City Inlet.
From the vantage point of a lifeguard, it's a
long hot summer. Beach Patrol member David
Zemo arrives well armored for his first day of
work on Memorial Day weekend (above).

From surf to Boardwalk, the beach at the inlet
hits peak performance on Fourth of July
weekend. In 1989, 340,000 visitors set an
Ocean City holiday weekend record (preceding pages).

The beach means business, from professional photographers who snap and sell summer memories (right) to concessions for beach umbrellas (above). Nearly eight million visitors a year-with an economic impact exceeding two billion dollars-make Ocean City Maryland's tourism leader. Summer brings the largest crowds, more than 300,000 people a week on average, but some three million people visit throughout what was once called the off-season.

Getting a lift or taking a pounding is all in a day's play on the beach. As yesterday's teenagers return as adults with their own children, Ocean City continues its tradition as a family resort.

The beach renews a promise of youth in dreams played out in tide pools, sand castles, and surf.

"A sandbar there jacks up the surf," explains Jon Ashton (above), who makes some of the region's best boards at Ashton Surf Design in Berlin, Maryland. "I couldn't afford to buy boards because I was spending more time surfing than working," he says. "So I started making them."

"There's not a month we don't surf here," says resident Ray Rickett. "Thirty-five degrees is about as cold as the water gets in the winter, and wet suits keep us warm." Known for fast tubular waves, Ocean City hosts nearly a dozen competitions a year. In summer the designated surfing beach rotates daily by street number. But before 10 a.m. (left) and after 5:30 p.m. it's surfer's choice, and the 48th Street beach is a favorite (preceding pages).

"I want to build the world's largest sand castle." That's the dream of Adam Showell, who helped raise Maryland's largest sand castle in 1989. A laughing gull surveys the architectural detail of the 30 - foot - high palace. The goal for SandCastle Fest 1990 is a 40 - foot - tall sculpture illuminated by lasers. " The world record is now 55 feet," says Showell. "It takes sponsors, but someday we'll reach 60 feet."

Trumpeting their approval, spectators greet three hours of fire trucks, floats, and marching bands in Ocean City's largest parade, the rowdy finale of the annual June convention of the Maryland State Volunteer Fireman's Association.

In a tough day of competition for Best Body on the Beach at the Ocean Club, this entry placed third (right).

Standouts at the July Mid-Atlantic Lifeguard Championships-with events such as the two-mile soft-sand run (preceding pages) and swimming and rescue-board competitions-the Ocean City Beach Patrol saved 3,000 people in 1989 and alerted 54,000 others about to slip into trouble. "We're not lifeguards, we're surf-rescue technicians," says George Schoepf, the captain who trains the close-knit 135-member group. "It's a skilled job, and we put our lives on the line every time we go into the water."

Sleep alfresco all you want between 6 a.m. and 10 p.m. But if you've tucked in for the night on the beach-with illegal brews in your shoes-expect a wake-up call from the police.

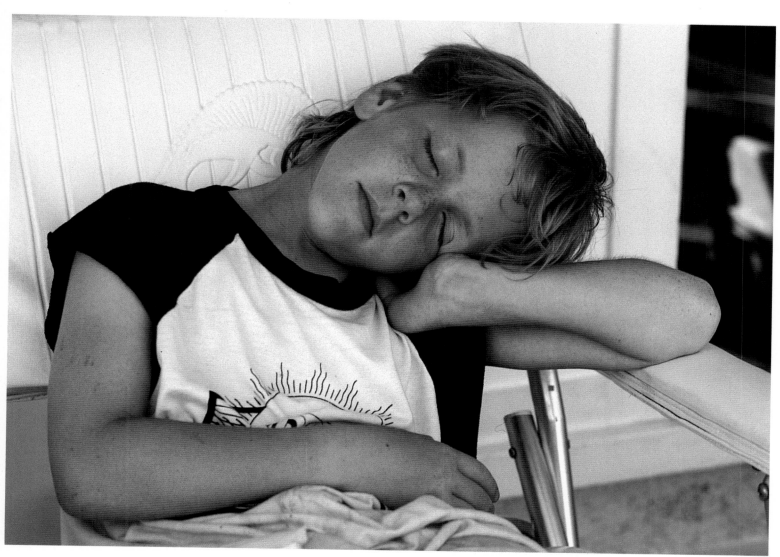

Dynamic beach volleyball reflects the sports-minded 1980s, when the city's recreation program boomed.
Fields at the 58-acre Ocean City Recreation Complex now lure major softball tournaments.

Glimmering back bays, up to five miles wide yet no more than six feet deep, make Ocean City and neighboring Assateague Island prime territory for windsurfing and catamaran sailing. Sinepuxent Bay stretches behind Assateague; Assawoman Bay and Isle of Wight Bay lap Ocean City. "But locally we just call them the bays," says Peck Miller, who sponsors races through his store, Sailing, Etc. The back bays also attract jet skiers, though ocean waves offer a wilder ride (following pages).

It's never insulting to tell Bill Ochse to go fly a kite. Unfurling a wind sock on the beach, the exuberant founder of the world's largest kite business sets out a trademark of The Kite Loft, a chain he started in Ocean City in 1975. Whimsical and traditional models fly at the September Sunfest Kite Festival (above), which Ochse has sponsored since 1981. Taking note of these lofty pursuits, Maryland governor William Donald Schaefer named Ocean City the Kite Capital of the World in 1988.

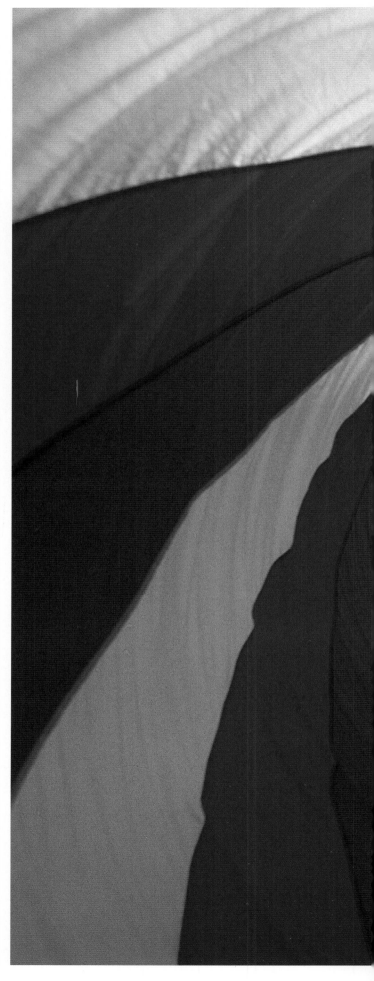

Awakening both body and soul, a couple practices the ancient Chinese exercise of tai chi at dawn (above).

Feet massaged by the surf, today's beach walkers would appreciate the sentiment of an 1892 visitor: "The temperature of the sea was perfect, and nothing but the failing twilight called us back to the shore."

JESUS WELCOMES ALL

"I'm an artist and I'm a minister," says Randy Hofman, who has spread the gospel in Ocean City's sand since 1980. "I like to reassure people that God loves us." Each evening's sculpture takes about three hours, longer for the elaborate Palm Sunday tableau (left). A crowd in front of the Plim Plaza (top) watches him shape his eight-hour masterpiece, the Last Supper. "That one is the toughest, and it's the favorite," says Hofman, ordained in Salisbury's Delmarva Evangelistic Church. "If no drunks jump on it, it still looks fresh the next morning."

Labor Day weekend at Ocean City (preceding pages) contrasts with that on Assateague Island (left) and illustrates a story of two island siblings gone separate ways. Ocean City had long dominated tourism when the 1933 hurricane divided Fenwick and Assateague Island at the inlet. A violent 1962 winter storm dashed resort development on Assateague, and in 1965 the federal government set aside the 37-mile-long barrier island as Assateague Island National Seashore. Wild ponies (above) have roamed here since the late 17th century. New developments in horse birth control help rangers keep the pony population at about 150 to prevent overgrazing.

Arcades, fast food, and souvenirs beckon on the southern stretch of the Boardwalk, paved in concrete in the 1950s.
But wooden planks and more peaceful strolling reign for most of the three-mile promenade.

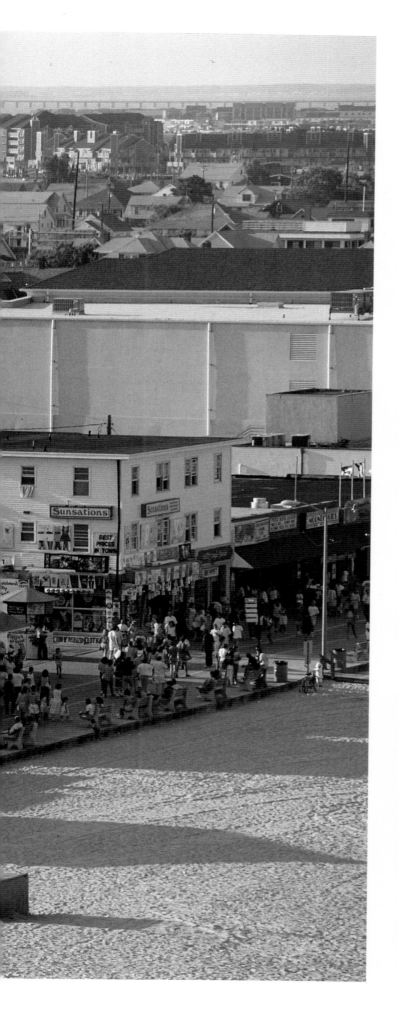

NEON RUBBER SUNGLASSES $2⁹⁸

"I have a unique approach to fine art-it should be fun."
Joe Kro-art's philosophy is reflected in every inch of his
Ocean Gallery World Center. "Many galleries are set
up to tell people what good taste is," he says. "Ours is
just the opposite." Its exterior a work of art in progress,
the landmark on the Boardwalk at Second Street holds
the most art per square foot in the world, maintains
Kro-art. "I applied to Guinness, but it's a new category
so there's no competition." Kro-art went into business
selling his own paintings on the Boardwalk in the early
1960s. Though he added the hyphen, the last name is
real. "It's Austrian."

"People make at least one pilgrimage to the Boardwalk no matter where they're staying," says Officer William Kerns (above), a veteran observer on this beat. "And on the Fourth of July (left) everyone lets their hair go. I've seen it all." The building now housing the futuristic space game called Photon was a dance pavilion when Kearns joined the Ocean City Police Department in 1971. Storms, fires, and changing fashion have altered the look of the Boardwalk many times since it was first laid down in the1880s. But some things remain the same: Though rebuilt in 1978, Dolle's Candyland has been doing business at this site for 80 years.

Food for the fun of it-Boardwalk fare has no other requirement. Pulling saltwater taffy at Dolle's Candyland (left), Rudolph Dolle takes pride and delight in running the business his grandfather acquired in 1910. Made without a drop of salt water, the candy got its name on the Atlantic City Boardwalk in the 1880s.

"Then there's Thrasher's, which is all some people know about boardwalk food, and all one needs to know if french fries are as important to your life as they should be." Reviewing Boardwalk cuisine, *Washington Post* food critic Phyllis Richman explained why people stand in dauntingly long lines for Thrasher's fries. It began in 1929 when Georgia transplant Joe Thrasher rented a new store at the head of the pier and started frying potatoes in peanut oil. "It's a cultural icon," says Thrasher's current owner, Ocean City businessman Charles "Buddy" Jenkins. "We operate it with no deviation from the original process." Delivery trucks (left) off-load the 100-pound sacks of potatoes that Thrasher's buys by the train car.

A first summer job for many Ocean City natives is selling seashells brought ashore by winter storms.

The resort has always inspired business pluck. When Mary B. Quillin opened the Lankford Hotel at Eighth Street in 1924, "people told her it was ridiculous to build so far up the beach-no one would come," says Quillen's great-niece Sally Rutka, who runs the still-thriving inn on the Boardwalk today.

Sparkling in name and product, the Star of Maryland crafts glass figures and colors its Boardwalk window with stained glass. Second-hand treasures come under scrutiny at the Convention Center's weekend flea market.

"Practically all the visitors are Marylanders," a writer observed of Ocean City in the early 1940s. In today's greater demographic mix, a third of the tourists-such as Lucy Hahn of Scranton (top)-hail from Pennsylvania.

Surf rescue boats and pieces of the past fill the Ocean City Life-Saving Station Museum. One of the city's oldest buildings, the 1891 structure was itself rescued from demolition by history-minded residents in 1977 and moved eight blocks from Caroline Street to the Boardwalk at the inlet. Responsible for saving ship-wreck victims, the U.S. Life-Saving Service-merged into the U.S. Coast Guard in 1915-first opened a station in Ocean City in 1878. It's men also served as lifeguards and firemen in the resort's early years. Largest fish ever caught in Maryland, the 1,210-pound tiger shark displayed in front of the museum was landed 27 miles off shore in 1983.

Summer memories are made of these: the cooling burst of a post-ocean shower, the exhilaration of fireworks on the Fourth of July. Illuminating the pier and its amusement parks, the celebration also recalls a local anniversary: Ocean City's first major hotel opened on July 4, 1875.

Hot stuff of another era, classic Chevys and hundreds of other cars fill the Convention Center parking lot in September for the World of Wheels. A major factor in increasing Ocean City's winter tourist trade, the Convention Center opened in 1970.

Ranked as one of the best in the country, Skateboard Park at Third Street and St. Louis Avenue hosts the National Skateboarding Association Eastern Finals.

Short on precision, long on enthusiasm, twirlers strut inthe Maryland Volunteer Fireman's Parade. Some 4,000 firemen from the mid-Atlantic region attend Ocean City's largest convention each June (preceding pages).

The Department of Public Works mobilizes for the summer invasion; money collected from 1,950 city parking meters helps pay costs. Ocean City tourism generates more than $92 million in tax revenue.

Practicing for an 8 p.m. post time, driver and standardbred work out at Delmarva Downs, a summer harness racetrack and year-rou

"I try to ride every morning," says Mayor Roland "Fish" Powell, born and raised on Dorchester Street. As in most of Ocean City's early families, his father was a fisherman and his mother operated a summer rooming house. "The women ran Ocean City in those days," says Annie Gilligan Bunting, here with her late son Fred (below). She built and managed five apartments while her husband served in the Coast Guard. Wad Spring (opposite) reportedly brought the first car to Ocean City.

"The heart and soul of youthful intensity," says Ocean City Magazine of Samantha's Nite Club, a hot stop on the summer circuit. Stepping out before the judges, an entry vies for prize money in a best-body contest.

Whirling dervishes of light, the rides on the Ocean City Amusement Pier (following pages) include a Ferris wheel nearly 110 feet tall.

On the slow float, Riptide Water Park on the Pier supplies the old fashioned summer pleasure of tubing.

On the fast track, the roller coaster at Jolly Roger Amusement Park accelerates from zero to sixty in less than two and a half seconds (preceding pages).

Living up to its name, Riptide Water Park offers thrills of speed among its nine different attractions on the Pier. First opened in 1907, the Pier was hailed as "one of the greatest improvements Ocean City has made."

A haunted house on the Pier and a barker at Jolly Roger Park continue an Ocean City amusement-park tradition started by Daniel Trimper in 1890. Still operated by his descendants, Trimper Rides recently restored its spectacular 1902 carousel (right), originally powered by a steam engine. The park's first merry-go-round was pulled by a large white horse.

Five miles from the ocean, amusement-park boats jump waves at Grand Prix in West Ocean City (above).

Go-carts tackle curves and embankments on the tracks of Speedworld at Jolly Roger Amusement Park (right). Launched in 1964 by Ocean City entrepreneur Charles "Buddy" Jenkins, the resort's largest amusement park now covers more than 36 acres.

In Isle of Wight Bay (following pages), Bahia Marina rents the real things for fishing or cruising.

Casting at sunrise, a surf fisherman may
land bluefish or sea trout. Flounder is a
likely catch off the Chicago Avenue bay
pier. A tuna lured from a deep ocean canyon
intrigues a young dock watcher.

"People used to look down on shark fishing - then they realized how much fun it is,"says Captain Mark Sampson of the Ocean City Sharkers. Aboard his charter boat, *Fish Finder* (above and top), Sampson encourages tag-and-release, since sport and commerical fishing have lowered shark numbers.

A 514-pound tiger shark (left) brought in on another boat was caught and kept for eating.

A brace of dolphin and a trio of white marlin express the rewards of Ocean City sportfishing. The resort's fame as the White Marlin Capital of the World dates from 1939, when 171 were hooked on one day. Prize money of 50,000 dollars draws more than 200 boats in early August for the White Marlin Open, the largest bluewater fishing tournament on the East Coast.

The quest for blue crabs sends people to any lengths. Outfitted for serious crabbing, Frank DiFatta (above) lands as many as six dozen a day in Isle of Wight Bay. Says his mother, "We have to rope him to get him home."

Sixty miles offshore over the Washington Canyon, Captain Jeff James (right center) and the crew of the *Patricia J.* retrieve and rebait 300 lobster pots on each 24-hour-long trip they make during the April to December season. Local restaurants serve the bounty.

A dramatic facelift changed the island's profile in the early 1970s when more than a dozen high-rise condominiums sprang up in north Ocean City. Unguarded speculation burst the condominium bubble in 1974, though stable ventures continued. By the end of the decade, housing units in Worcester County had increased 118 percent; Ocean City's growth accounted for most of it. In the 1983 real-estate boom, a development trendsetter was Harbour Island in Isle of Wight Bay (above).

The kitchen hustles to serve capacity crowds of 1,400 at Phillips Crab House, an Ocean City institution launched by Shirley Phillips as a take-out venture in 1957. All-American waitresses are Phillips' trademark, and the coveted summer jobs offer " a wonderful family experience," recalls former employee Jody Mayo. "We lived together, played together, and even had a yearbook (preceeding pages)."

A city in itself, Sea Watch condominium earns its name in oceanfront balconies (right). Stairway travel is less intimidating at the five-story Sandy Square (above).

High-rising north Ocean City takes a long look down from the 21-story Atlantis condominium (above) and oversees the Coastal Highway's summer rush (right) from the 26-story Quay condominium - narrowly bested as the city's tallest building by the Century I. Anticipating growth, Ocean City in 1965 extended its city limits from 45th Street to the Delaware border, now 146th Street.

Hometown Ocean City, a neighborhood on Assawoman Bay (above) houses some of the city's 8,500 year-round residents. Warning beacon to ships from 1859 to 1979, the Fenwick Island Lighthouse (right) lies just over the border in Delaware. Called the Transpeninsular Line, the east-west boundary of Maryland and Delaware links up with the Mason-Dixon Line-the states' north-south border-midway through the Delmarva Peninsula. Completed in 1760, the survey of these lines ended decades of legal wrangling between the Maryland Calverts and the Penns of Pennsylvania. It was most likely William Penn who granted a Delaware tract here in the 1680s to Captain Thomas Fenwick, who gave his name to Ocean City's barrier island.

Now protected by state law, back bay wetlands nurture blue crabs, oysters, small fish, and wading birds.   During the 1960s hundred

acres of marsh were filled in for development.

Telescope trained on the Ocean City Inlet, Hal Wierenga surveys "one of the bird-watching hot spots of Maryland." Food stirred up by turbulent tides attracts terns, gulls, and pelicans, and is a magnet for winter visitors along the Atlantic flyway such as eider and harlequin ducks. " And in the spring and fall you can do a lot of bird watching right in the streets of town, " says Wierenga. "The bushes are jumping with warblers." A year-round wading · bird resident, a great blue heron in Isle of Wright Bay pauses in a ditch dug to give fish that eat mosquito larvae better access to the marsh.

Oriental sika deer were released on Assateague Island in the 1920s by boy scouts who may have raised the exotic species as a project. Today's population in the high hundreds is controlled by legal hunting.

Dusting goose decoys after a rare Thanksgiving snow, Tron Thorton tends a West Ocean City field leased to hunters seeking waterfowl that winter along the Atlantic flyway (preceding pages).

Midwinter snow isn't front page news in Ocean City, but strolling along a frosted Boardwalk is a feature attraction (preceding page

"We get at least one good snowstorm every year,"says Jimmy Hockersmith (right). No deterrent to surfer Steve Hentschel (below), snow complicates the life of clammer Sonny Layton. Top earner in Ocean City's commercial fishery, clamming is subject to heavy federal regulation. Even if the weather is bad, a boat may go to sea rather than forfeit its assigned clamming day, "That's when the wives bite their nails," says vetern fisherman Dave Martin.

134

An El Dorado of food and entertainment, a bayside restaurant glows at sunset. Questing for treasure, a metal-detector buff scans beneath the Pier (following pages).

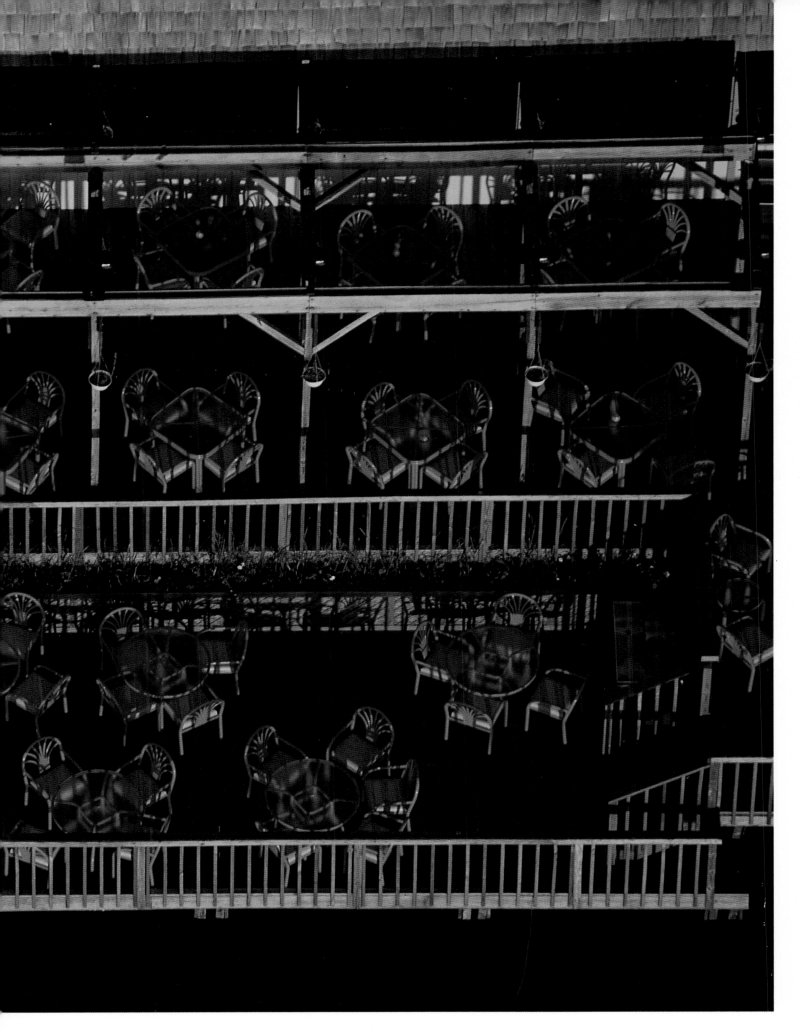

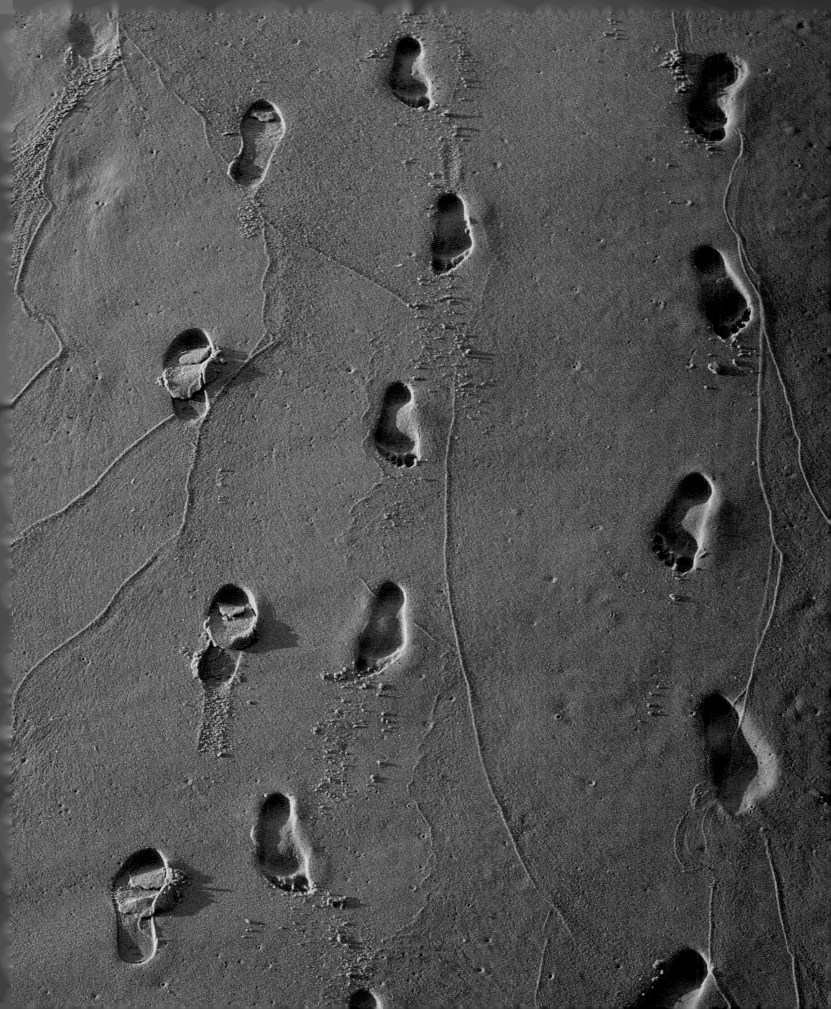

Farewell messages and final strolls mark the sunset of summer. Sharing the joy of daybreak, a couple bends the rules to perch on a Beach Patrol stand (preceding pages). Though much of the city now remains open during winter months, the advent of fall still brings retrospection. "People do a lot of growing up in Ocean City," says the sand-sculpting minister, Randy Hoffman. "When you're on vacation you have a chance to se yourself better, Ocean City is a nice place to punctuate those transititions in your life."

This book was made possible
by the generous support
of the
Bank of Ocean City . . .
Ocean City's Bank Since 1916.

Design by Marti Betz

Printed in Hong Kong by Everbest Printing Co., Ltd.
through Four Color Imports, Ltd., Louisville, Kentucky

PHOTOGRAPHS BY KEVIN FLEMING

Cover, endpapers, title page, pages: 1, 12-13, 14-15, 28, 36, 37 (upper), 38-39, 40, 41, 44, 46, 47, 48,
49 (upper), 50-51, 52, 53, 54, 55, 56, 57, 58, 61 (upper left, lower), 64 (lower), 66 (upper left), 69 (lower), 90, 91, 92,
94 (lower), 97, 112, 113, 115, 119, 120-121, 124-125, 136-137, 138-139, 142

PHOTOGRAPHS BY DAVID TROZZO

Pages: 10-11, 16, 17, 18, 19, 20, 21, 22, 23, 24-25, 26, 27, 29, 30, 31, 32,33,34-35, 37(lower), 42-43, 45, 49 (lower),
59, 60, 61 (upper right), 62, 63, 64 (upper), 65, 66 (upper right, lower), 67, 68, 69 (upper), 70, 71, 72, 73, 74-75, 76, 77, 78, 79, 80-81,
82, 83, 84, 85, 86-87, 88-89, 93, 94 (upper), 95, 96, 98-99, 100, 101, 102, 103, 104, 105, 106, 107, 108, 109, 110, 111,
114, 116, 117, 118, 122, 123, 126-127, 128-129, 130-31, 132, 133, 134-135, 140-141, 143

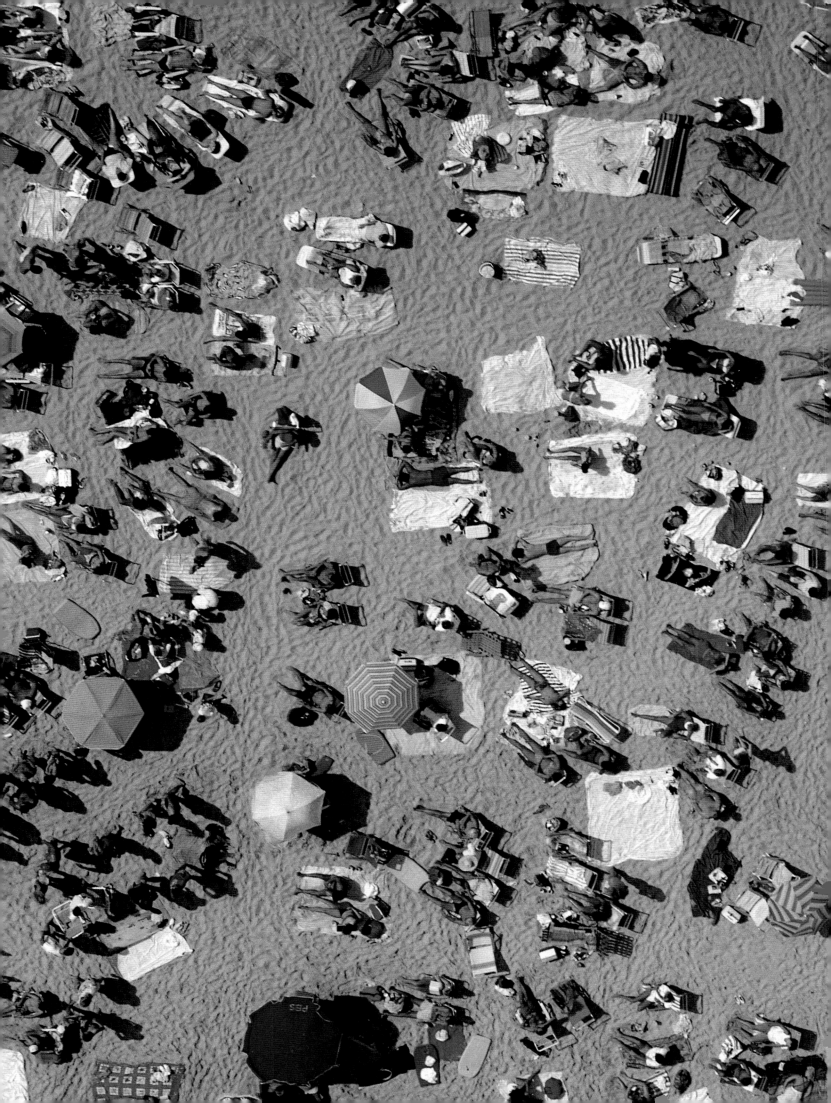